This standard format verbal reasoning book contains 850 que
detachable answer sheets. Each test can be completed in under one hour.
It is a compilation of all the work in Learning Together's *Verbal Reasoning Books 1 & 2.*

Verbal Reasoning Tests is book 1 in a set of 2 and the succeeding book is called *More Verbal Reasoning Tests.*

The book is an excellent aid in preparing children for their 11+ or 12+ examinations.
It can also be used in preparing children for grammar school, independent and private
school selection tests and contains work suitable for the CEM tests.
(These tests vary depending on the Local Education Authority or school. You should check
requirements with your Local Education Authority or school.)

The authors are experienced teachers and tutors who have developed and used these tests
extensively in the classroom over a number of years.

Working through these tests will provide children with experience of formal testing while
at the same time helping them to become more familiar with various types of verbal
reasoning question.

The Learning Together range of Verbal Reasoning books complements their range of
Non-Verbal Reasoning books and their *"How to do" Non-Verbal* and *Verbal Reasoning Step by
Step* books.

Stephen McConkey MA(Ed) BEd(Hons)
Tom Maltman BA

Published 2015
ISBN 978-1-873385-36-4

LEARNING TOGETHER

ADVICE AND INSTRUCTIONS ON COMPLETING THESE TESTS

1. There are 85 questions in each test. Make sure you have not missed a page.

2. Start at question 1 and work your way to question 85.

3. If you are unable to complete a question leave it and go to the next one.

4. Do not think about the question you have just left as this wastes time.

5. If you change an answer make sure the change is clear.

6. Make sure you spell correctly.

7. You may do any rough work on the test paper or on another piece of paper.

8. Each test should take approximately 50 minutes.

9. When you have finished each test mark it with an adult.

10. An adult may be able to explain any questions you do not understand.

TEST 01

SCORE _____

A B C D E F G H I J K L M N O P Q R S T U V W X Y Z

1. What is the sixth letter of the alphabet?   (_____)

2. Which day begins with the letter fourth from the end of the alphabet?   (_____)

3. Which letter appears most often in the word DISCIPLINE?   (_____)

4. Which letter appears in PEAR but not in APPLE ?   (_____)

5. Which of these words would come last if they were put in alphabetical order?

    CAULIFLOWER   CUCUMBER   CABBAGE   CARROTS   (_____)

Find the word which means the same or almost the same as the word outside the brackets.
Look at this example: TINY means (HUGE HEAVY <u>SMALL</u> OLD)
The word SMALL is underlined because it means the same as TINY.

6. OLD   means   (BRAVE   YOUNG   ANCIENT   FAT)

7. GRUMBLE   means   (HUNGRY   THUNDER   MOAN   NOISY)

8. BRAG   means   (CARD   GYPSY   CLOTHES   BOAST)

9. CONSTRUCT   means   (HOUSES   LEGO   BUILD   BRIDGE)

10. BASHFUL   means   (FRETFUL   HAPPY   TEARS   SHY)

In the next questions the first three words in each line are alike in some way. One word in the brackets is also like these three words.
Look at this example: PINK   ORANGE   BROWN (colour <u>red</u> apple tree)
RED is underlined because it is also a colour.

In the following questions underline ONE word each time.

11. OIL   COAL   PEAT   (gas   grass   soil   sand)

12. COPPER   IRON   GOLD   (plastic   bottle   lead   rubber)

13. CABBAGE   PEA   CARROT   (tomato   tulip   turnip   beef)

14. DOLLAR   FRANC   CENT   (money   pound   coin   cheque)

15. FOAL   CALF   PUP   (cow   sow   cub   mare)

A B C D E F G H I J K L M N O P Q R S T U V W X Y Z

Complete these sequences by inserting the correct letter or number in the brackets.
Look at this example: 1 2 3 4 (_5_)
5 completes the sequence so it goes in the brackets.

16. A, C, E, G, (_____)

17. A, Z, B, Y, (_____)

18. 7, 11, 15, 19, (_____)

19. D, F, I, M, (_____)

20. 34, 27, 22, 19, (_____)

One word does not belong in each of these lists. Underline it.
Look at this example: HORSE COW PIG <u>HAMSTER</u> SHEEP

HAMSTER is underlined because it is not a farm animal.

21. INFANTRYMAN GUNNER DOCTOR CAVALRYMAN SOLDIER

22. RIND COVER SKIN LAYER CUT

23. TRANQUIL PEACEFUL SILENT CONTENT PROFITABLE

24. PAUSE PAUPER DELAY INTERVAL LULL

25. OCEAN SEA ISLAND LAKE RIVER

Ben is taller than Maya but smaller than Samuel.
List these three children starting with the tallest first.

tallest 26. (_____) 27. (_____) 28. (_____) smallest

Write one word in each bracket so that the sentence makes sense.
Look at this example: The child (...CUT...) his finger.
Other words may also make sense.

29. I am 2 years younger (_____) my sister.

30. We set the table (_____) knives and forks.

31. You must train hard (_____) get fit.

32. The table was (_____) with white paint.

33. The door (_____) a brass letter box.

Find the correct order for the lists and underline the MIDDLE word.
Look at this example: FINGER   WRIST   SHOULDER   NECK   <u>ELBOW</u>
Elbow is underlined because when the words in the list are put in order (finger, wrist, elbow, shoulder, neck), elbow is in the middle.

34. CRAWL   SPRINT   RUN   WALK   STAND

35. EDITOR   CUTE   BLACK   ARABLE   DANGER

36. $^5/_4$ $^3/_4$ $^1/_4$ $^2/_4$ $^4/_4$

37. 6   8   10   3   7

38. X   Y   O   P   Q

39. 17 and another number equal 33. What is the other number?   (_____)

40. $^1/_4$ of 12 plus $^1/_5$ of 15 equals?   (_____)

41. 4 balls cost £6. How much for 5?   (_____)

42. Three boys share 25 apples so that one has 6 apples and
another has 12 apples. How many apples has the third boy?   (_____)

43. If ten men can paint a mansion in 5 days how many men would
be needed to paint it in one day?   (_____)

Complete these sequences:

A B C D E F G H I J K L M N O P Q R S T U V W X Y Z

44.   23,   21,   18,   14   (_____)

45.   17.5, 18.0   18.5   19.0   (_____)

46.   Z,   Y,   W,   T,   (_____)

47.   6,   9,   13,   18   (_____)

48.   AZ,   BX,   CV,   DT   (_____)

ALWAYS HAS: In these questions you have to underline one thing from inside the brackets that the thing outside the brackets ALWAYS HAS.

Look at this example:

A MAN always has a (<u>BRAIN</u>   SHOES   CHILDREN   DOG   WIFE)
Brain is underlined because a man always has a BRAIN.

Now try these and underline only one word.

49. A BUS always has   (DRIVERS   PASSENGERS   FARES   WHEELS   UPSTAIRS)

50. A DOG always has   (FUR   MASTER   KENNEL   PUPS   COLLAR)

51. A BIRD always has   (EGGS   NEST   CHICKS   FEATHERS   SEEDS)

52. A MAN always has a   (SHIRT   HEART   HOUSE   CAR   GLOVES)

53. A WEDDING always has   (CHURCHES   CAKES   PEOPLE   RINGS   PRAYERS)

54. A HILL always has   (GRASS   TOP   SHEEP   TREES   RIVER)

55. A KNIFE always has a   (SHEATH   SHARPNESS   FORK   BLADE   COVER)

In the questions below, one word does NOT belong in each list.

Look at this example: LEAD GOLD COPPER ZINC <u>CHALK</u>
Chalk is underlined because it is not a metal and so it does NOT belong in the list.

Underline the word which does NOT belong in each list.

56. MAHOGANY   TEAK   OAK   STEEL   PINE

57. NYLON   RAYON   PLASTIC   SILK   ACRYLIC

58. TRILBY   BERET   SOU'WESTER   BOWLER   SCARF

59. NAILS   DRILL   PLIERS   CHISEL   HAMMER

60. TUG   SUBMARINE   LINER   FERRY   BATTLESHIP

OPPOSITES:

In each of the following sets of brackets, underline ONE word which is the OPPOSITE, or nearly the OPPOSITE, of the word outside the brackets.

61. SAD   (SORROW HAPPY TEARS CRY LAUGH)

62. LOSE   (LAST MISS SECOND FIRST WIN)

63. SHARP   (KNIFE BLUNT SCISSORS NEEDLE BLADE)

64. FOE   (ENEMY SOLDIER FRIEND PERSON TEACHER)

65. YOUNG   (CHILD MAN BABY ADULT OLD)

66. OVER   (THROUGH AROUND UNDER BESIDE BEHIND)

67. LAUGH   (SORROW TEARS SING SHOUT CRY)

ALIKE: (Similar)
In each list below find the TWO words which are most alike in some way.
Look at this example: (<u>ASH</u> WOOD <u>OAK</u> PLANK DOOR)
ASH and OAK are both underlined because they are both trees.

Now try these questions - remember to underline TWO words which are similar.

68. BLUE   DRESS   FROCK   SHIRT   TROUSERS

69. DRIVER   PASSENGER   CONDUCTOR   MAN   PILOT

70. HAND   EYE   TEETH   HAIR   FOOT

71. WATCH   HOUR   CLOCK   TIME   BELL

72. CELLOTAPE   ADHESIVE   STICKY   MUDDY   GLUE

73. CAR   BUS   BICYCLE   LORRY   TRUCK

Three boys Thomas, Blake and Wiliam go to the cinema and sit side by side.
Thomas is not beside Blake. Blake sits on the extreme right.
List the boys from left to right.

74. (_____) left

75. (_____)

76. (_____) right

There are four shops in a town. One is painted black, one white, one purple and the other is painted green. The black and purple shops are large, the others small. The black and white shops sell flowers, the others sell sweets.

77. What colour is the large sweet shop?   (_____)

78. What colour is the small sweet shop?   (_____)

79. What does the purple shop sell?   (_____)

80. What size is the white flower shop?   (_____)

81. What does the white shop sell?   (_____)

82. What number is 6 more than $\frac{1}{2}$ of 8?   (_____)

83. What number is 3 less than $\frac{1}{3}$ of 12?   (_____)

84. What number is 5 more than 13 plus 15?   (_____)

85. What number divided by 4 gives 2 less than 12?   (_____)

TEST 02

SCORE _____

1. Which letter occurs in RUGBY and in BALL?   (_____)

2. Which letter occurs once in PUPIL and once in PRIMARY?   (_____)

3. Which letter occurs once in SCORE and once in UNDERLINE?   (_____)

In the questions below TWO words must change places so that the sentences make sense. Underline the TWO words that must change places.

Look at this example: **The <u>wood</u> was made of <u>table</u>.**

4. My permission has child to go to camp.

5. Any regarding queries this letter should be sent to my office.

6. You to advised are bring boots.

7. The river had flooded the rain.

8. Six letters later the weeks arrived.

A, B, C, D and E are five aeroplanes.
E is due EAST of C. C is due EAST of B.
C is due NORTH of D and due SOUTH of A.

9. Which aeroplane is furthest WEST?   (_____)

10. Which aeroplane is furthest NORTH?   (_____)

11. Which aeroplane is furthest EAST?   (_____)

12. Which aeroplane is furthest SOUTH?   (_____)

Complete these sequences.

13. 12, 20, 28, 36,   (_____)

14. 27, 26, 24, 21,   (_____)

15. 2, 4, 12, 48,   (_____)

16. 401, 423, 445, 467,   (_____)

17. 14, 17, 22, 29,   (_____)

Complete these sequences. The alphabet is printed to help you.

A B C D E F G H I J K L M N O P Q R S T U V W X Y Z

18. B, E, G, J,   (_____)

19. C, F, K, R,   (_____)

20. Y, W, T, R,   (_____)

21. XY, VW, TU, RS,   (_____)

22. ZB, YD, XF, WH,   (_____)

In each sentence below a word has 3 letters missing. The letters are next to each other and they spell a word. Write the missing words in the brackets.

Look at this example: Begin sentences with CAAL letters.   (P I T)
The complete word is CAPITAL.

23. The driver FED his car with diesel.   (___ ___ ___)

24. The holiday APMENTS were near the beach.   (___ ___ ___)

25. DED for tickets was so great that we were unable to go. (___ ___ ___)

26. Mum always says that Christmas is an EXSIVE time.   (___ ___ ___)

27. Good outside LIGHG at night should help to prevent break-ins. (___ ___ ___)

In each sentence below the letters of the word in capital letters have been jumbled up. Re-arrange the letters to get the correct word.

Look at this example: **A NOBRI is a bird.**   **(<u>ROBIN</u>)**

28. RISPA is a capital city in Europe.   (_____)

29. One of the countries in Europe is MUGBEIL.   (_____)

30. You use a REAMMH to bang in nails.   (_____)

31. The river MAESHT flows through London.   (_____)

32. A mechanic uses a RNPSANE to tighten nuts.   (_____)

Charlie, Dylan, Jessica and Jade are four children who each take part in three of the following four sports: hockey, swimming, golf and badminton. Only Jade does not play golf.
Dylan and Jade are the only two children who can swim. Charlie, Jessica and Jade play hockey.

33. Which girl can swim?   (_____)

34. Which boy plays golf but can't swim?   (_____)

35. What sport does everyone take part in?   (_____)

36. What sport does Dylan not play?   (_____)

37. Charlie plays hockey, badminton and what else?   (_____)

In a certain code CONFIDENTIAL is written as XYPTZWRPSZBO.
Write the following coded words in their proper form.

38. ORPSZO (_____)   39. PYSRW (_____)   40. PRRW (_____)

Write the following words in their coded form.

41. LATE (_____)   42.DEAL (_____)   43.FIDDLE (_____)

In the paragraph below five words are missing. Choose the most appropriate words from the lists below. One word from list A fills the space at A, one word from list B fills the space at B and so on.

Underline the words you choose.

Plants are sometimes starved of (A) and this causes the plant to go (B). Most plants need water to grow (C). Some plants such as the cacti do not receive (D) water as they live in the desert. Their (E) skin helps them to save water.

44.	45.	46.	47.	48.
A	B	C	D	E
SOIL	RED	UP	GALLONS	GREEN
AIR	GREEN	DOWN	MUCH	COLD
WATER	FLOWERS	GREEN	COLD	PALE
GRASS	OLD	STRONG	FRESH	SLIMEY
POTS	BROWN	WEAK	MORE	SHINY

In a group of five children, Lily is not as old as Ben or Teddy but is older than Saanvi and Bella. Saanvi is not the youngest and Teddy is not the oldest.
List the children starting with the oldest.

49. (_____) Oldest

50. (_____)

51. (_____)

52. (_____)

53. (_____) Youngest

A FOUR letter word is hidden in each of the sentences below. The hidden words begin at the end of a word in the sentence and finish at the start of the next word.

Write the hidden words in the brackets

Look at this example:
Time <u>and</u> tide wait for no one.   **(MEAN)**

54. Put the flask in the bag.   (_____)

55. It rained all over the weekend.   (_____)

56. These attacks must stop.   (_____)

57. Light the fire very carefully.   (_____)

58. The satellite moved in orbit.   (_____)

59. Do not waste money on me.   (_____)

Each word below can be made into a new word by leaving out one letter and without altering in any way the order of the letters.
Write the letter that can be left out in the brackets.

Look at this example: CLEAN leave out (__C__) gives LEAN

60. UNIT   (_____)   61.   HORSE   (_____)

62. TOY   (_____)   63.   SOAK   (_____)

64. SOLDIER   (_____)   65.   NOTE   (_____)

The words in each question 66 - 70 can be allocated to one of the groups A - E. The words in the lists are alike in some way. Write, in the brackets, the letter of the list that each word belongs to.

Look at this example: FRENCH belongs to list (__A__) because all the words are nationalities.

66. SENTINEL (_____)   67. SWISS   (_____)   68. CLOG (_____)

69. ALERT   (_____)   70. CONTENT (_____)

A	B	C	D	E
POLISH	TRANQUIL	KEEPER	SLIPPER	VIGILANT
NORWEGIAN	QUIET	GUARD	SHOE	ATTENTIVE
GREEK	PEACEFUL	CUSTODIAN	BOOT	CAREFUL
ITALIAN	RELAXED	WARDEN	WADER	CONSCIOUS
DUTCH	CAREFREE	CARETAKER	SANDAL	OBSERVANT

The word in capitals has three letters missing. The letters that are missing form a three letter word on their own. Write that three letter word in the brackets.

Look at this example: London is a _____ital city. (___CAP___)

71. A number of words together is a SEN___CE.   (_____)

72. The man waited ____IENTLY for his wife.   (_____)

73. A mountain may have a very high ____K.   (_____)

74. The sun was ____DEN by clouds.   (_____)

75. A cellar is BE___ ground level.   (_____)

Here are the dates of birth of five people.

A. 29/2/12   B. 23/11/12   C. 27/6/13   D. 20/7/14   E. 1/7/13

76. Which person is the youngest?   (_____)

77. Which person is the oldest?   (_____)

78. Which person has a proper birthday every four years?   (_____)

79. Which two people were born on two consecutive months,
    though in different years?   (_____&_____)

80. E was born on a Friday. What day was C born on?   (_____)

The table below shows the dates of attendances and number of attendances of children and adults at Chester Zoo. A code letter is given for each attendance.

TRIP	A	B	C	D	E
DATE	23/5/07	23/6/08	24/5/07	27/12/06	12/6/08
NO. OF ADULTS	201	237	197	183	211
NO. OF CHILDREN	190	210	205	197	193

81. Which attendance occurred in winter?   (_____)

82. Which two attendances occurred on consecutive days
    in the same year?   (_____) and (_____)

83. On which date were there 18 less children than adults
    at the zoo?   (_____)

84. Which trip had most visitors?   (_____)

85. Which trip had least visitors?   (_____)

TEST 03

SCORE _____

1. Which letter occurs only once in STATISTIC but twice in STATISTICAL? (_____)

2. Which letter occurs 3 times in MASTERFULNESS but only once in MASTERMIND? (_____)

3. Which letter occurs twice in INFIRMARY, once in HOSPITAL but not at all in NURSE? (_____)

4. What number is 7 less than 8 plus $\frac{1}{2}$ of 12? (_____)

5. Tea costs half as much as coffee in a cafe. Two teas and one coffee cost £2.
   How much is coffee? (_____)

**In the questions below TWO words must change places so that the sentences make sense.
Underline the TWO words that must change places.
Look at this example:**　　　　The <u>wood</u> was made of <u>table</u>.

6. You take always should care with fireworks.

7. Racing sport can be a dangerous cars.

8. The snow white the ground with a covered carpet.

9. The early worm catches the bird.

10. The subtraction from 9 of 12 gives 3.

The table below gives some information about the addition of numbers in the left hand column to those in the top row.

Complete the table correctly.

11. 12.	+		24	
	12	21	36	37
13.	17		41	42
14. 15.			39	40

In each line below write, in the brackets, one letter which completes the word in front of the brackets and the word after the brackets.

Look at this example: ROA (D) OOR   D completes ROAD and begins DOOR.

16.   AM (_____) OWER   17.   PART (_____) AWN

18.   MINE (_____) INED   19.   PROPERT (_____) OLK

20.   SPEA (_____) EASON

In each line below underline TWO words, ONE from each side, which together will make one correctly spelt word. The word on the left always comes first.

Look at this example: **BLACK** ALL TOP   AND **BIRD** BOY

21.	BOY	LIE	SO		GIRL	MAN	HOOD
22.	ASH	HOME	BALL		LAND	OR	GO
23.	HEN	FISH	COCK		SEA	BUT	ROACH
24.	TEA	STAR	IN		TRAIN	SIDE	BUS
25.	AT	GOLF	BACK		LAST	BUT	BONE

In the following questions a letter can be taken from the first word and put into the second word to form TWO new words. Write both NEW words.

Look at this example. THEN   TANK   (TEN)   (THANK)

The H moves from THEN to TANK and makes the new words TEN and THANK.

26. SLACK   WORD   (_____)   (_____)

27. GREED   BEAN   (_____)   (_____)

28. SOLDIER   GRAN   (_____)   (_____)

29. HEART   DEER   (_____)   (_____)

30. HERD   RAFT   (_____)   (_____)

In each of the following sentences one word has had 3 letters removed from it. The missing letters are next to each other and they spell a word.

Write the missing 3 letter words in the brackets.

Look at this example: **The cat jumped up and STED to run. (ART)**

31. There is SOHING wrong with the television.   (_____)

32. The driver drove BACKDS into the parking space.   (_____)

33. Plant GTH slows down during the winter.   (_____)

34. We had an ARGUT and did not speak for a while.   (_____)

35. The team MANR decided which players would play on Saturday.   (_____)

In questions 36-40 the three words A, B and C are in alphabetical order. The word at B is missing and you are given a dictionary definition. Write the correct word in the space.

Look at this example: A)   **FL__AP__ _ _**
                              B)   **(F L A R E) Distress signal from a boat**
                              C)   **FLASH**

36. A)   FJORD
     B)   (_ _ _ _)   Material with a country's colours on it.
     C)   FLAKE

37. A)   PROFESS
     B)   (_ _ _ _ _ _)   To gain money or benefit.
     C)   PROGRAMME

38. A)   AFFECT
     B)   (_ _ _ _ _ _)   To have enough money to buy something.
     C)   AFTER

39. A)   GANNET
     B)   (_ _ _)   A mountain pass.
     C)   GARAGE

40. A)   SUTURE
     B)   (_ _ _ _)   Cotton wool used to mop up blood.
     C)   SWAG

In the following questions choose ONE word from each set of brackets to make a sensible sentence. Underline your 2 words.

Look at this example:

Cup is to (Drink, <u>Saucer</u>, Spoon) as Bucket is to (Metal, Water, <u>Spade</u>)

41. Never is to (Happy, Always, End)   as Few is to (None, Count, Many)

42. Sun is to (Time, Mirror, Light)   as Fire is to (Fuel, Heat, Coal)

43. Knife is to (Fork, Cut, Sharp)   as Thread is to (Needle, Wood, Knot)

44. Pen is to (Pencil, Write, Ruler)   as Brush is to (Duster, Bristle, Sweep)

45. Tap is to (Apt, Water, Pat)   as Live is to (Bad, Evil, Vile)

In the following questions letters take the place of numbers. Complete the sums and give the answers as letters.

Look at this example:
A = 7 B = 2 C = 4 D = 1 E = 5   B + C + D =   Letter <u>A</u>

46. A = 3 B = 5   C = 7   D = 15 E = 20   C + A + B =   Letter _____

47. A = 1 B = 10 C = 7   D = 4   E = 6   C - D + A =   Letter _____

48. A = 3 B = 6   C = 8   D = 5   E = 2   B + C - D - A =   Letter _____

49. A = 3 B = 4   C = 6   D = 8   E = 7   D - A + C - B =   Letter _____

50. A = 7 B = 8   C = 13 D = 14 E = 20   E - B + A - C + D = Letter _____

In the paragraph below five words are missing. Choose the most appropriate words from the lists below. One word from list A fills the space at A, one word from list B fills the space at B and so on.

Underline the words you choose.

Admiral Beaufort invented a scale used to estimate wind (A). He was an admiral in the (B). He based his scale on (C) the effects of the wind. He invented the scale for use at (D). It is still in use (E).

51.	52.	53.	54.	55.
A	B	C	D	E
CALM	AIRFORCE	PASSING	WAR	SOMETIMES
HEIGHT	WAR	VISIBLE	PEACE	TO-DAY
SPEED	POLICE	HARSH	LAND	TO-MORROW
LENGTH	ARMY	OCCASIONAL	HOME	THEN
TIME	NAVY	GENTLE	SEA	ALTHOUGH

In a certain system of counting three symbols are used £, L and *

2	is written as	£
5	is written as	L£
8	is written as	LL£
10	is written as	LLL*

In this system of counting how would the following numbers be written?

56. 3 (_____)   57. 11 (_____)   58. 12 (_____)

59. 6 (_____)   60. 17 (_____)

A man is facing South West. He then turns ³/₄ of a turn clockwise, ¹/₄ of a turn anti-clockwise and finally a ³/₄ turn clockwise.

61. What direction is he now facing?   (_____)

62. He then turns ³/₄ of a turn anti-clockwise. What direction is he now facing?   (_____)

63. What direction is directly opposite the direction he is now facing?   (_____)

64. Through how many degrees must he turn to face his original direction?   (_____)

In each question 65 - 70 the numbers in the second column are formed from the numbers in the first column by using a certain rule. A different rule is used in each question. Put the correct answer opposite the arrow.

65. 5 $\longrightarrow$ 20   66. 8 $\longrightarrow$ 2   67. 40 $\longrightarrow$ 9

6 $\longrightarrow$ 30   12 $\longrightarrow$ 6   48 $\longrightarrow$ 11

7 $\longrightarrow$ 42   15 $\longrightarrow$ 9   68 $\longrightarrow$ 16

8 $\longrightarrow$ 19 $\longrightarrow$ 76 $\longrightarrow$

68. 2 $\longrightarrow$ 11   69. 5 $\longrightarrow$ 7   70. 100 $\longrightarrow$ 180

3 $\longrightarrow$ 30   6 $\longrightarrow$ 9   80 $\longrightarrow$ 140

4 $\longrightarrow$ 67   12 $\longrightarrow$ 21   60 $\longrightarrow$ 100

5 $\longrightarrow$ 17 $\longrightarrow$ 50 $\longrightarrow$

Complete each sequence by inserting the correct number in the brackets.

71.   5.6,   4.2,   2.8,   1.4,   (_____)

72.   7,   7,   14,   42,   (_____)

73.   7,   12,   12,   7,   17,   (_____)

74.   4,   103,   202,   301,   (_____)

75.   110   291,   472,   653,   (_____)

76.   216,   125,   64,   27,   (_____)

77.   36,   49,   64,   81,   (_____)

The first word can be changed into the second word in three stages, by replacing one letter at a time and each time making a proper word.
Look at this example:

TAKE   (LAKE)   (LIKE)   LIVE

There may be more than one way of doing this question.

78. PIPE   (_____)   (_____)   HILL

79. WIDE   (_____)   (_____)   SING

80. MILE   (_____)   (_____)   SINK

81. HILL   (_____)   (_____)   MOLE

Using the numbers 3, 5, 7 and 9 once only in each question fill in the spaces in any way which makes the statements correct.

Look at this example: (3 x 7) + (9 - 5) = 25

82. (_____) + (_____) + (_____) - (_____)   = 6

83. (_____ X _____) + (_____ X _____)   = 66

84. (_____ + _____) - (_____ + _____)   = 0

85. (_____ - _____) + (_____ - _____)   = 8

TEST 04

SCORE _____

1. Which letter occurs twice in NARROWNESS but only once in ROADWAY? (_____)

2. Which letter occurs twice as often in CONVERSE as it does in CONVEX? (_____)

3. Which letter occurs twice in CHOCOLATE, twice in COCONUT but only once in COMPETITION? (_____)

4. Half of a number is 6 more than the product of 3 and 6. What is in the number? (_____)

5. A boy spent ¹/₆ of his money on sweets and ¹/₄ on comics. If he finished with £3.50 how much had he at the start? (_____)

In the sentences below TWO words must change places in order for the sentences to make sense. Underline the TWO words which must change places.

Look at this example: The <u>wood</u> was made of <u>table</u>.

6. A narrow over led road the mountains.

7. Was plane the delayed by fog.

8. The birthday had card a clown on it.

9. This boat was to last the leave port.

10. A red delight at night is a shepherd's sky.

The table below gives information about the addition of the numbers in the top row to those in the left hand column. Complete the table correctly.

+	27	36	
	32	41	
4		40	11
	40	49	20

11,

12. 13.

14.

15.

TEST 04 PAGE 1

In each line below write in the brackets one letter which completes the word in front of the brackets and the word after the brackets.

Look at this example: **ROA (D) OOR**

16. INHAL (_____) JECT

17. FLA (_____) OLE

18. JEWE (_____) UMP

19. INFIR (_____) INSTREL

20. PATC (_____) AGGLE

In each line below underline TWO words, ONE from each side, which together make ONE correctly spelt word. The word on the left always comes first.

Look at this example: <u>**BLACK**</u> ALL TOP AND <u>**BIRD**</u> BOY

21.	AT	HER	SO		OUT	TEND	BAR
22.	ROW	FOOT	SOW		BARN	PATH	CAN
23.	BLACK	TIT	COW		BARN	BAT	OUT
24.	TART	FLAG	BY		HEN	ON	OUT
25.	TEST	CAR	AT		AGE	GIRL	TEMPT

In the following questions a letter can be taken from the first word and put into the second word to form TWO new words. Write both NEW words.

Look at this example.   THEN   TANK   (TEN)   (THANK)

The H moves from THEN to TANK and makes the new words TEN and THANK.

26. FLARED   HER   (_____)   (_____)

27. BEGAN   BRIDE   (_____)   (_____)

28. BLEACH   EAR   (_____)   (_____)

29. BRASS   ASH   (_____)   (_____)

30. FALLOW   BEE   (_____)   (_____)

Put these words in the order that you would find them in a dictionary.

SUPERVISE   SUPERSEDE   SUPERB   SUPPLE   SUPERIOR

31. (_____)   32. (_____)   33. (_____)

34. (_____)   35. (_____)

Complete the sequences by inserting the correct numbers in the brackets.

36.   9.3,   7,   4.7,   2.4,   (_____)

37.   0.6,   1.2,   2.4,   4.8,   (_____)

38.   8,   12,   18,   26,   (_____)

39. (17,58)   (30,45)   (43,32)   (56,19)   (_____,_____)

40.   0.4   1.2   3.6   10.8   (_____)

41 - 45. In the paragraph below five words are missing. Choose the most appropriate words from the lists. One word from list A fills the space at A, one word from list B fills the space at B and so on.

Underline the words you choose.

Darren was always (A). At the first opportunity he would open the (B) door and take (C) from its icy interior. His (D) loved to bake apple tarts and she gave some to Darren, and told him not to touch the rest, which she put in the fridge. She was very (E) when she caught her son taking tart from the fridge.

41. A	42. B	43. C	44. D	45. E
THIRSTY	HOUSE	TART	COUSIN	HAPPY
TIRED	CUPBOARD	ICE CREAM	SISTER	ARROGANT
HUNGRY	WARDROBE	BREAD	FATHER	ANGRY
DIRTY	KITCHEN	SAUSAGES	BROTHER	PLEASED
READING	FRIDGE	JELLY	MOTHER	AMBITIOUS

The following table gives the number of bottles of milk, lemonade and orange juice that three children drank in one year.

	MILK	LEMONADE	ORANGE JUICE
AVNI	171	88	57
RYAN	129	86	52
GEORGE	114	90	58

46. Which child drank half as many bottles of orange juice as George drank bottles of milk? (_____)

47. Which child drank three times as many bottles of milk as bottles of orange juice? (_____)

48. Which child drank most bottles of orange juice? (_____)

49. For which child was the difference between the number of bottles of lemonade drunk and the number of bottles of orange juice drunk the greatest? (_____)

50. Which child drank one and a half times as many bottles of milk as bottles of lemonade? (_____)

In the questions below one word can be put in front of the other words to form four new words. Write the correct word in the brackets.

Look at this example: FLY   PROOF   WORKS   MAN   (FIRE)

51. LONG   HIND   LOW   FRIEND   (_____)

52. MADE   WRITING   SOME   CUFFS   (_____)

53. COVER   ROOM   CLOTHES   TIME   (_____)

54. LOOK   REACH   SIDE   GOING   (_____)

55. CRAFT   GUN   LINE   MAIL   (_____)

56. HEAD   TIME   HAUL   BOARD   (_____)

A B C D E F G H I J K L M N O P Q R S T U V W X Y Z

In a certain code some words are written as shown.

EXAMPLE   is written as   **FYBNQMF**

PHRASE   is written as   **QISBTF**

STRAIGHT   is written as   **TUSBJHIU**

What would these coded words be in English?

57. HSBQFT   (_____)   58. SFBNT   (_____)   59. SBQJFS   (_____)

Write these words in code

60. HEIGHT   (_____)   61. PAPER   (_____)   62. STAR   (_____)

Underline the word in the brackets that the object outside the brackets always has.

Look at this example:

A cat always has   **(KITTENS, MILK, FISH, <u>FUR</u>)**

63. A horse always has   (SADDLE, REINS, HAY, HOOFS)

64. Water is always   (COLD, WARM, TEPID, WET)

65. A shoe always has   (LACES, STRAPS, SOLE, LEATHER)

66. Sandra is always a   (GIRL, LADY, NAME, AUNT)

67. A room always has   (LIGHTS, WINDOWS, FLOOR, PLUGS)

68. A sewing machine always has a   (NEEDLE, MOTOR, PATTERN, HANDLE)

Four children, Pari, Sophia, Adam and Sam all had a birthday today.
In one years time Sam will be the age Pari is now.
Adam is half of Sophia's age and is three years younger than Sam.
Sam is 11 years old.

69. What age is Pari now?   (_____)

70. What age is Sophia now?   (_____)

71. What age will Adam be when Sam is 15 years old?   (_____)

72. What age is Adam now?   (_____)

In each question 73 - 78 the numbers in the second column are formed from the numbers in the first column by using a certain rule. A different rule is used in each question.
Put the correct answer opposite the arrow.

73.				74.				75.			
14	→	12		4	→	22		6	→	70
12	→	11		5	→	31		10	→	110
10	→	10		6	→	42		25	→	260
8	→			7	→			47	→	

76.				77.				78.			
144	→	9		64	→	4		2	→	12
121	→	8		27	→	3		3	→	17
100	→	7		8	→	2		6	→	32
9	→			1	→			8	→	

In a certain system of counting

3	is written as	)
4	is written as	) <
5	is written as	) /
6	is written as	))

79. 1 (_____)

80. 2 (_____)

81. 8 (_____)

82. 7 (_____)

83. 10 (_____)

84. 9 (_____)

85. 11 (_____)

TEST 05

SCORE _____

1. Which letter occurs twice in the word AMERICA and twice in AUSTRIA?   (_____)

2. Which letter occurs three times as often in EXASPERATE as it does
   in CUTANEOUS?   (_____)

3. Which letter occurs only once in HABERDASHER but twice in DRESSER?   (_____)

4. One fifth of a number plus 12 equals half of 40. What is the number?   (_____)

5. I get a total of 19 when I add a third of 18 to a certain number. What is the number?   (_____)

In the sentences below TWO words must change places in order for the sentences to make sense. Underline the TWO words which must change places.

Look at this example: The _wood_ was made of _table_.

6. The driving cold made them rain and miserable.

7. A lot of harsh died during the birds winter.

8. Skiing is winter popular a sport.

9. Public give a great service to the hospitals.

10. A bird in the bush is worth two in the hand.

The table below gives some information about the addition of numbers in the left hand column to those in the top row.

Complete the table correctly.

11. 12.	**+**	**5.3**		
13.		**9.8**	**17.2**	**9.2**
14. 15.		**8.7**	**16.1**	

In each line below write, in the brackets, one letter which completes the word in front of the brackets and the word after the brackets.

Look at this example: **ROA (D) OOR**

16.   PO   (_____) OWN   17.   STOR   (_____) EEN

18. SATI   (_____) OBLE   19.   FOO   (_____) ABLE

20. STEA   (_____) EGAL

In each line below underline TWO words, ONE from each side, which together make ONE correctly spelt word. The word on the left always comes first.

Look at this example: **<u>BLACK</u>** ALL TOP   AND **<u>BIRD</u>** BOY

21. HOST   GRASS   TREE   GREEN   AGE   AT

22. OUT   IN   ON   TRAIN   PAT   AUDIBLE

23. IF   AND   SO   IT   UP   NO

24. SON   BE   BY   TOWN   TEST   AT

25. LET   MAN   BOY   AT   IF   OR

In the following questions a letter can be taken from the first word and put into the second word to form TWO new words. Write both NEW words.

Example. THEN   TANK   (TEN)   (THANK)

The H moves from THEN to THANK and makes the new words TEN and THANK.

26. INSERT   FONT   (_____)   (_____)

27. MONTHS   MAY   (_____)   (_____)

28. SHOES   LET   (_____)   (_____)

29. FRICTION   BEAST   (_____)   (_____)

30. THANK   CASE   (_____)   (_____)

Five politicians A, B, C, D, and E have offices at the five corners of this pentagon.
The corners are numbered 1 - 5.
E's office is opposite D's which is furthest east.
No-one has an office further north than C.
B is not to the east of A.

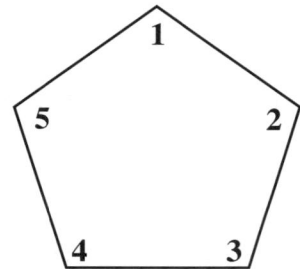

31. Which politician has his office at number 1?   (_____)

32. Which politician has his office at number 2?   (_____)

33. Which politician has his office at number 3?   (_____)

34. Which politician has his office at number 4?   (_____)

35. Which politician has his office at number 5?   (_____)

In questions 36 - 42 the three words A, B and C are in alphabetical order. The word at B is missing and you are given a dictionary definition. Write the correct word in the space.

Look at this example: A) **FLAP**
                       B) (**F L A R E**) **Distress signal from a boat.**
                       C) **FLASH**

36. A) SHACKLE
    B) (_ _ _ _ _ _)   Patch of shade.
    C) SHAKE

37. A) PROSPER
    B) (_ _ _ _ _ _ _)   To keep from harm.
    C) PROUD

38. A) EXCLUDE
    B) (_ _ _ _ _ _)   To forgive, to free from blame or duties.
    C) EXECUTE

39. A) TREAT
    B) (_ _ _ _ _ _)   To make three times as much.
    C) TREE

40. A) WAIST
    B) (_ _ _ _)   To be in a place in readiness.
    C) WAKE

41. A) FLEECE
    B) (_ _ _ _ _)   A number of ships.
    C) FLESH

42. A) MELON
    B) (_ _ _ _)   To become liquid from solid.
    C) MEMORY

Complete these sequences by inserting the correct number in the brackets.

43.   9.6,   8.2,   6.8,   5.4,   (_____)

44.   2,   5,   11,   23,   (_____)

45.   89.1,   29.7,   9.9,   3.3,   (_____)

46.   8,   27,   64,   125,   (_____)

47.   127,   118,   111,   106,   (_____)

48.   2,   10,   50,   250,   (_____)

49.   10.4,   12.5,   14.6,   16.7,   (_____)

In the paragraph below five words are missing. Choose the most appropriate words from the lists below. One word from list A fills the space at A, one word from list B fills the space at B and so on.

Underline the word you choose.

The (A) of bells rang out (B) the people to church. It was snowing (C) and everything was covered in a fine sprinkle of snow. The December air was sharp and people were coming to celebrate (D) in a church which had been (E) in a festive manner.

50. A	51. B	52. C	53. D	54. E
CLANG	CALLING	HEAVILY	EASTER	BUILT
PEEL	SHOUTING	HARD	CHRISTMAS	COVERED
PEAL	TELLING	SLOWLY	LENT	DECORATED
COVER	MAKING	LIGHTLY	HALLOWE'EN	DESIGNED
RATTLE	TALKING	QUICKLY	MASS	INFECTED

In each question 55 - 60 the numbers in the second column are formed from the numbers in the first column by using a certain rule. A different rule is used in each question.
Put the correct answer opposite the arrow.

55. 2 ⟶ 4   56. 3 ⟶ 3   57. 12 ⟶ 12
    3 ⟶ 9   4 ⟶ 8   20 ⟶ 16
    4 ⟶ 14   5 ⟶ 15   40 ⟶ 26
    5 ⟶   6 ⟶   44 ⟶

58. 2.4 ⟶ 0.6   59. 3 ⟶ 30   60. 217 ⟶ 208
    3.6 ⟶ 0.9   4 ⟶ 68   326 ⟶ 317
    4.4 ⟶ 1.1   5 ⟶ 130   456 ⟶ 447
    6.4 ⟶   6 ⟶   538 ⟶

Underline the word in the brackets that the object outside the brackets ALWAYS has.

Look at this example: A cat always has   (KITTENS, MILK, MOUSE, <u>FUR</u>)

61. A garden always has   (ROSES, SOIL, HEDGES, PATHS)

62. A bat always has   (YOUNG, CAVE, FUR, BELFRY)

63. A village always has   (BUSES, RAILWAYS, SCHOOLS, BUILDINGS)

64. A book always has   (PAGES, WORDS, PICTURES, INDEX)

65. A chicken always has   (EGGS, NEST, ROOSTER, FEATHERS)

66. A plant always has   (ROOTS, FLOWERS, STEMS, BUDS)

Paula is now three times as old as Jane will be in 5 years time.
In 5 years Paula will be 29 years old.

67. What age is Paula now?   (_____)

68. What age is Jane now?   (_____)

69. What age will Jane be in 8 years?   (_____)

In a certain system of counting

5 is written as X
7 is written as XY
11 is written as XXZ

13 is written as XXW
19 is written as XXXV

In this system of counting, how are these numbers written?

70. 2 (_____)   71. 8 (_____)   72. 14 (_____)   73. 3 (_____)

A B C D E F G H I J K L M N O P Q R S T U V W X Y Z

In a certain code   **ZEBRA**   was written as   **CHEUD**

HORSE   was written as   **KRUVH**

POLAR BEAR   was written as   **SRODU EHDU**

Write these words in code.

74. MONKEY   (_____)   75. RABBIT   (_____)

Decode these words

76. ILQFK   (_____)   77. FDJH   (_____)

A man cashes a cheque for £12.98 and receives the money in the smallest possible number of each note and coin shown below. How many of each does he receive?

(Use only the notes and coins given.)

78. £5 notes   (_____)   79. 50p coins (_____)   80. 10p coins (_____)

81. 5p coins   (_____)   82. 1p coins (_____)

Each shape is drawn on 16 small squares which are all the same size and which join together to form one large square. Calculate what fraction of each large square is shaded.

83.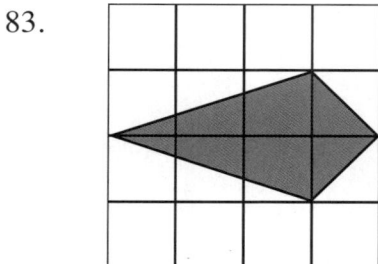

(_____)

84.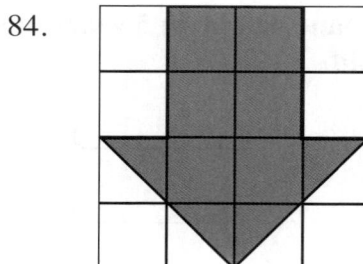

(_____)

85.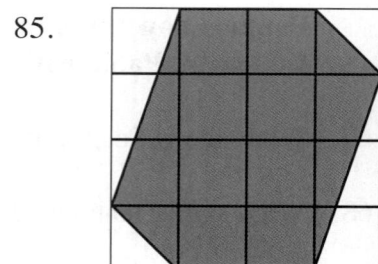

(_____)

TEST 06

SCORE _____

1. Which letter appears once in TUMBLED but twice in RESTAURANT? (____________)

2. Which letter appears once in ROMANTIC but not at all in FORMATION? (____________)

3. Two times ten is the same as a number multiplied by four. What is the number? (____________)

4. A banana and 2 apples cost 86p. Two bananas and 2 apples cost £1.16.
How much is an apple? (____________)

In the questions below TWO words must change places so that the sentences make sense. Underline the TWO words that must change places.

Look at this example: The <u>wood</u> was made of <u>table</u>.

5. The television was breakfast on after switched.

6. A car outside down broke the garage.

7. Take great care crossing when a busy road.

8. Not a pen I can without do my homework.

9. Making a foolish decision is sometimes hasty.

The table below gives some information about the subtraction of numbers in the top row from numbers in the left hand column. Complete the table.

10.	—	2.6		4.9
11, 12.	7.8			2.9
13, 14.	5.3		1.2	

In each question below write in the brackets a letter which will complete both the word in front of the brackets and the word after the brackets.

Look at this example.   ROA (D) OOR

15.   WIS   ( )   EAR   16. SEVE   ( )   ANGE   17. BOT   ( )   EIR

18.   SPEL   ( )   RACE   19. TIC   ( )   ING

In each line below a word from the left-hand group joins one from the right-hand group to make a new word. The left-hand word comes first.
Underline the chosen words.

Look at this example.

CORN	FARM	TIME	OVER	FIELD	YARD
20. STAR	ONLY	STIR	DEN	PAD	TING
21. PACK	SPOKES	TOP	AGE	OVER	WHEEL
22. TIN	CAP	BIN	BAG	GO	LID
23. COT	MODEL	FOR	LED	RAT	RING
24. UNDER	HOUSE	OPEN	FIRE	HOLD	OTHER

Four children A, B, C and D sat a test in school. A scored 5 more marks than B and 8 less than C. D scored 37, which was 22 less than B scored.

How many marks did each child score?

25. A scored   (_____)   26. B scored (_____)

27. C scored   (_____)   28. D scored (_____)

In each of the following questions one word can be put in front of each of the four given words to form a new word. Write the correct word in the brackets.

Look at this example.

board	berry	out	bird	(BLACK)

29. take   stand   line   ground   (_____)

30. break   come   cry   burst   (_____)

31. table   less   keeper   piece   (_____)

32. ways   board   wards   light   (_____)

Four brothers Adam, Ben, Charlie and David each own a car. Adam and Ben have sports cars and the others have hatchbacks. Ben and David have new cars and the others own second-hand cars. Only the cars owned by Adam and David have a radio.

33. Who has a new hatchback with a radio?   (_____)

34. Who has a hatchback which is not new and has no radio?   (_____)

35. Who has an old sports car with a radio?   (_____)

36. Has anyone a second-hand hatchback without a radio?   (_____)

37. Who has a new sports car without a radio?   (_____)

Complete each sequence by writing the correct number or numbers in the brackets.

38.   3   4   6   10   (_____)

39.   1.5   2.75   4   5.25   (_____)

40.   100   64   36   16   (_____)

41.   8.8   7.4   6   4.6   (_____)

42.   520   432   344   256   (_____)

43.   (30,45)   (37,43)   (44,41)   (51,39)   (_____ , _____)

In the following questions the letters of words have been jumbled up. A clue is given to help you find the word each time.

Look at this example:

	IATSDUM	Sports Ground	**STADIUM**
44.	AVRACAN	Mobile home	(_____)
45.	TLAIOSHP	Where sick people are treated	(_____)
46.	IELPMP	Small swelling on skin	(_____)
47.	NGNILTHIG	Electrical storm	(_____)
48.	SEVERER	Drive backwards	(_____)
49.	ROAHCDR	Area where fruit trees grow	(_____)

In the sentences below there are 5 words missing. From the lists A to E choose the MOST SUITABLE words to complete the sentences. Choose a word from list A to fill space A, a word from list B to fill space B and so on.

<u>Underline the chosen word in each group</u>.

Gasping for breath the runner made a (A) desperate (B) for the tape. (C) he collapsed (D) on the road, officials covered him with a blanket and then (E) him to a nearby hall.

50.	51.	52.	53.	54.
A	B	C	D	E
most	chase	Why	weary	sent
hopeful	go	Quickly	unconscious	pointed
great	spurt	But	tired	directed
last	bounce	As	over	ushered
big	fling	For	down	carried

The two sets of numbers on each line go together in a similar way. Write the missing number each time.

Look at this example: (7 → 14 → 16) (9 → 18 → 20) Double number and add 2

55. (32 → 40 → 10)   (4 → 12 → ____)

56. (3 → 9 → 27)   (5 → 25 → ____)

57. (36 → 18 → 17)   (14 → 7 → ____)

58. (5 → 7 → 49)   (9 → 11 → ____)

59. (4 → 8 → 18)   (6 → 12 → ____)

Two words inside the brackets have similar meanings to the words outside the brackets. Underline the two words each time.

Look at this Example: Horse, Pig, Cat   (Falcon, Mouse, Snake, Trout, Badger)

60. Cabbage, Turnip, Carrot   (Cherry, Wheat, Cauliflower, Pear, Parsnip)

61. Barrel, Bucket, Bath   (Bottle, Basket, Bag, Box, Bowl)

62. Search, Look, Inquire   (Find, Seek, Report, Explore, Lead)

63. Teach, Educate, Instil   (Coach, Learn, Instruct, Study, Swot)

64. Vacant, Free, Available   (Unfurnished, Occupied, Fill, Empty, Unoccupied)

Some letters from the words in capitals have been used to make other words. Underline the TWO new words that have been made each time.

Look at this example:

CONVENIENT	<u>Tonic</u>	Video	Notion	<u>Voice</u>
65. PRACTICE	Erase	Trace	Create	Crate
66. GLADIATOR	Tailor	Great	Tiger	Gloat
67. DISCIPLE	Edits	Plaice	Slide	Piles
68. OPERATION	Train	Rather	Parent	Nations
69. MYSTERIOUS	Yeast	Mouse	South	Items

RHOMBUS   TRAPEZIUM   PARALLELOGAM   RECTANGLE   KITE
The above are all quadrilaterals and are defined below.
Beside each definition write the name of the shape.

70. The four sides are equal in length but the angles are not right angles.   (_____)

71. Made up of 2 pairs of parallel lines. The opposite sides are equal and all the angles are right angles.   (_____)

72. There are 2 pairs of equal sides which are not opposite to each other   (_____)

73. A quadrilateral with one pair of sides parallel.   (_____)

74. Opposite sides and angles equal. Two pairs of parallel lines.   (_____)

The table below shows the number of pupils in a school who attended after-school activities.

	Year 4	Year 5	Year 6	Year 7
Folk Dancing	10	6	5	3
Football + Hockey	7	13	15	19
Cookery	6	8	5	8
Choir	7	5	6	4

75. Which activity becomes more popular as children get older?   (_____)

76. Which activity becomes less popular as children get older?   (_____)

77. Which activity is the second most popular?   (_____)

78. Which activity has exactly half as many taking part as another one has?   (_____)

79. It started to rain and all the football and hockey players were divided equally among the other clubs. How many were then at folk dancing?   (_____)

In a number system

1	is written as ~\	2	is written as ~\~\
3	is written as ><	4	is written as ><~\
6	is written as ><><	8	is written as ><>< ~\~\
10	is written as []		

Which numbers are represented by the following?

80. >< ><~\   (_____)   81. [] >< ~\~\   (_____)

82. [] >< >< ><   (_____)   83. [] [] >< >< ~\   (_____)

84. [] [] [] >< >< ~\~\   (_____)   85. [] [] [] [] [] ><~\~\   (_____)

TEST 07

SCORE _____

1. Which letter occurs once in UTTERANCE, twice in THROUGHOUT
   and three times in AUGUSTUS?   (_____)

2. Which letter, that does not occur in the word PRESENTABLE,
   occurs twice in DIMENSION?   (_____)

3. What number is three times the half of 8 multiplied by six?   (_____)

4. What is the difference between seven times nine and eight multiplied by five?   (_____)

5. I get a total of 20 when I add half of 18 to a quarter of a certain number.
   What is that number?   (_____)

When completed the table below gives the answers when the numbers in the left-hand column are subtracted from the numbers in the top row.

Complete the table correctly.

	—	9.7	12.2
6.	1.9	7.8	
7. 8.	4.4		
9. 10.		3.3	

In the questions below TWO words must change places so that the sentences make sense. Underline the TWO words that must change places.

Look at this example: The <u>wood</u> was made of <u>table</u>.

11. Many books can be learned from things.

12. Swim only safe waters in.

13. My uncle's brother is my nephew.

14. Our the is at the end of school road.

15. The runner fell lap in the last over.

In each question below write in the brackets a letter which will complete both the word in front of the brackets and the word after the brackets.

Look at this example: ROA (D) OOR

16. HAR ( ) ARLY   17. CRO ( ) ORD   18. POR ( ) ITE

19. ARI ( ) YE   20. GRAS ( ) HASE   21. BE ( ) UST

In each line below a word from the left-hand group joins with one from the right-hand group to make a new word. The left-hand word comes first. Underline the chosen words.

Look at this example: CORN   <u>FARM</u>   TIME   OVER   FIELD   <u>YARD</u>

22.	SCAR	DOWN	OAR		TANG	SIDE	LET
23.	OLD	UP	THIN		TEN	KING	DEN
24.	ALL	UPPER	THEM		MOST	SELF	TOGETHER
25.	PASS	IN	LET		TIME	PORT	ON
26.	FAR	BE	FULL		AM	HIDE	WEAR

£77.80 was made up using the smallest number of notes and coins shown below. How many of each were used?

27. £10 notes   (_____)   28. £5 notes   (_____)   29. £1 coins   (_____)

30. 50p coins   (_____)   31. 20p coins (_____)   32. 10p coins (_____)

Theo has more money than Jack and Leo, but less than Sam and Ben. Leo has less than Jack. Sam does not have the most money. List the 5 boys in order starting with the one who has the least money.

(least) 33. (_____) 34. (_____) 35. (_____) 36. (_____) 37. (_____) (most)

In the following sentences the words in capital letters have been jumbled up. Re-arrange the letters to form the correct words.

Look at this example: VESEN is a number.   (SEVEN)

38. Mother is KNOWIRG in the kitchen.   (_____)

39. I like tea and toast for SAKRBEAFT   (_____)

40. Cartoons on OLETESIVIN are fun to watch.   (_____)

41. The chocolate SIUTBICS melted in the sun.   (_____)

42. The BILARRY received many new books.   (_____)

43. The boy played the EROCNT in the brass band.   (_____)

In a certain month there were 5 Mondays and the 18th of the month was a Thursday.

44. If there were 5 Wednesdays, what was the date of the last day of the month?   (_____)

45. What day was the 29th of the month?   (_____)

46. What was the date of the second Friday in the month?   (_____)

47. How many Tuesdays were there in the month?   (_____)

48. Which of the months April, June or August could it have been?   (_____)

In each line below, the first word can be changed into the last word in three stages. Only one letter can be replaced at a time and proper words must be made each time.

Look at this example: tide   (ride)   (rode)   rope

49. dear   (_____)   (_____)   peep

50. lump   (_____)   (_____)   came

51. work   (_____)   (_____)   here

52. wood   (_____)   (_____)   hard

Five children, Ethan, Jacob, Stanley, Alfie and Logan have a school bag each. Ethan and Alfie have leather bags and the others have canvas ones. Only Ethan and Logan have bags with zips. Stanley and Ethan have outside and inside pockets in their bags. The others have only inside pockets.

53. Who has a leather bag with a zip?　　　　　　　　(＿＿＿＿＿＿)

54. What is the bag with an outside pocket and no zip made of?　　　　　　　　(＿＿＿＿＿＿)

55. Who has a canvas bag with a zip and no outside pockets?　　　　　　　　(＿＿＿＿＿＿)

56. Who has a canvas bag with no zip but with a full set of pockets?　　　　　　　　(＿＿＿＿＿＿)

57. How many children have bags that are not canvas, have no zips and have inside pockets?　　　　　　　　(＿＿＿＿＿＿)

Complete the following sequences. The alphabet is printed to help you.

A B C D E F G H I J K L M N O P Q R S T U V W X Y Z

58. C1F　　　D3G　　　E5H　　　F7I　　　　　　(＿＿＿＿＿＿)

59. CX　　　FW　　　IV　　　LU　　　　　　(＿＿＿＿＿＿)

60. Y　　　W　　　T　　　P　　　　　　(＿＿＿＿＿＿)

61. PBZ　　　OCY　　　NDX　　　MEW　　　　　　(＿＿＿＿＿＿)

62. Z　　　X　　　V　　　T　　　　　　(＿＿＿＿＿＿)

63. BAC　　　EDF　　　HGI　　　KJL　　　　　　(＿＿＿＿＿＿)

In each of the following questions, the numbers in the second column are formed from the numbers in the first column. A different rule is used for each question.

Write your answers in the brackets.

64. 4 ⟶ 15   65. 23 ⟶ 12
    6 ⟶ 35   35 ⟶ 18
    8 ⟶ 63   49 ⟶ 25
    10 ⟶ (_____)   55 ⟶ (_____)

66. 4 ⟶ 6   67. 144 ⟶ 14
    6 ⟶ 9   100 ⟶ 12
    10 ⟶ 15   81 ⟶ 11
    12 ⟶ (_____)   36 ⟶ (_____)

In each line below there are 3 words which change by following a rule.
Find the rule for each line and write the missing word.

Look at this Example: NOT - TON   LIVE - EVIL   STOP -   POTS

68. hasten - net   header - red   jersey - (_____)

69. cartridge - cage   elapse - else   figure - (_____)

70. surge - sure   tenant - tent   existent - (_____)

71. notable - tale   impassive - pave   mediaeval - (_____)

72. digger - dire   dowse - does   formula - (_____)

Complete the statements below by writing your answers on the lines.

73. (67 x 15) + (67 x 3) = 67 x (_____)

If 204 ÷ 12 = 17 then

74. (12 x 17) + (_____) = 215

In a code SLITHER is written as ABCDEFG and POUCH is written as HIJKE.

Which words are represented by the following code words?

75. EIJAF   (_____)   76. DCBFA   (_____)

77. HCDKEFG   (_____)   78. DEGCKF   (_____)

Write the following words in code.

79. COURSE   (_____)   80. LEISURE   (_____)

Using the numbers 2, 4, 6 and 7 ONCE ONLY in each question, fill in the spaces in a way that will make the statements correct.

Look at this example: (2 + 4) + (6 + 7) = 19

81. (_____ + _____)   X   (_____ + _____)   =   90

82. (_____ − _____)   +   (_____ − _____)   =   3

83. (_____ X _____)   ÷   (_____ − _____)   =   8

84. (_____ X _____)   −   (_____ X _____)   =   16

85. (_____ + _____ + _____)   X   (_____)   =   34

TEST 08

SCORE _____

1. Which letter occurs once in HEADINGS and twice in THOUGHTS? (____)

2. Which letter occurs twice in PHOTOGRAPHIC and once in INHARMONIOUS? (____)

3. Which letter occurs once in HOUSEHOLD, twice in MALADJUSTED
    and thrice in DIVIDENDS? (____)

**In the questions below TWO words must change places so that the sentences make sense.
Underline the TWO words that must change places.**

Look at this example: **The <u>wood</u> was made of <u>table</u>.**

4. The difficult asked a teacher question.

5. Thunder sound of the made me jump.

6. A cat dog's into the raced kennel.

7. Book pages are missing from the five.

8. Television is to very boring sometimes watch.

9. It's sleep for bed and time for time.

**In each question below write in the brackets a letter which will complete both the word in
front of the brackets and the word after the brackets.**

Look at this example.   **ROA (D) OOR**

10. HU   ( ) ORE   11. SIL   ( ) ILT

12. HUR ( ) ACE   13. STAR ( ) TEM

14. PART ( ) ULE   15. LAS   ( ) ERD

The table below gives some information about the addition of numbers in the left hand column to numbers in the top row.

Complete the table.

	+	7.5		3.5
16.				
17. 18.	3.8		4.2	
19. 20.	5.6			9.1

In the brackets, write the numbers required to complete the statements correctly.

21. (_____) + 19 = 45

22. 396 − 7 = (_____)

23. 5 X 45 = 5 X (_____) + (5 X 6)

24. 12 X (_____) = 6 X 124

25. 39 X 16 = (_____) + (39 X 15)

In each of the following words there are 4 successive letters which make a new word.
Write the new word in the brackets.

Look at this Example: PL<u>ENTI</u>FUL (LENT)

26. CUPBOARD   (_____)   27. FOREARM   (_____)   28. SHIVER   (_____)

29. BADMINTON (_____)   30. GAUNTLET (_____)   31. ATMOSPHERE (_____)

32. YEARNED   (_____)

In the sentences below there are 5 words missing. From the lists A to E choose the
MOST SUITABLE words to complete the sentences. Choose a word from list A to fill space A,
a word from list B to fill space B and so on. Underline the chosen word in each group.

The first (A) in the book was rather (B) but as the story (C) things became more exciting. The
hero (D) the (E) damsel and finally married her.

33.	34.	35.	36.	37.
A	B	C	D	E
pages	excited	went	fought	young
sentences	interesting	developed	imprisoned	only
chapter	bad	shows	saw	helpless
part	boring	continues	rescued	evil
story	short	unfolds	met	capture

At one time £1.00 was worth 224 Japanese yen.

38. How many yen would £2.50 have been worth?   (_____ Yen)

39. How many yen would £4.25 have been worth?   (_____ Yen)

40. In British money what was the value of 392 yen?   (__ £ _____)

41. In British money what was the value of 672 yen?   (__ £ _____)

In the following questions the letters of words have been jumbled up. A clue is given to help you find the word each time.

Look at this Example: IATSDUM   Sports Ground   **STADIUM**

42. IGNEPUN   Flightless sea bird   (_____)

43. HDUSOLRE   Joint at top of arm   (_____)

44. INVSRAH   Liquid which gives glossy appearance to wood   (_____)

45. NAMHELO   Opening in floor/sewer etc for person to pass through (_____)

46. CKUKSACR   Walker's bag worn on the back   (_____)

47. LFTIFAHU   To be loyal and true   (_____)

48. INCEDEVE   Information collected by police after a crime   (_____)

**One year February started and ended on the same day.
The 7th of the month was a Wednesday.**

49. How many Thursdays were there in the month?   (_____)

50. What was the date of the third Tuesday?   (_____)

51. What day was the 19th of February?   (_____)

52. What date was the last Saturday in January?   (_____)

53. What date was the second Tuesday in March?   (_____)

In the questions below give the next number in each series.

54.	3	4	7	12	(_____)
55.	2	6	18	54	(_____)
56.	21.5	17	12.5	8	(_____)
57.	8.8	8.2	7.6	7.0	(_____)
58.	4.83	5.34	5.85	6.36	(_____)

A child emptied her money box and had the following coins; four £1 coins, seven 50p coins, twelve 20p coins, nineteen 10p coins, fourteen 5p coins.

59. What was the total amount of money? (_£_____)

60. How much more would she need to buy a toy at £15.99? (_£_____)

61. By how much did the value of the 20p coins exceed the value of the 5p coins? (_£_____)

62. Would it have been possible to change the coins of lesser value than 50p to an exact number of £1 coins? (_____)

Number of children	?	15	8	6	2	1
Number of pets kept by each child	0	1	2	3	4	5

The table above shows the results of a survey on the pets kept by 40 children.

63. How many children kept no pets? (_____)

64. How many children with pets kept less than 3? (_____)

65. How many children kept more than 3 pets? (_____)

66. What fraction of the children did not keep pets? (_____)

In each question below a boy ALWAYS STARTS OFF facing NORTH WEST. (NW)

67. In what direction is he facing if he makes a quarter turn anti-clockwise? (_____)

68. In what direction is he facing if he makes a three-quarter turn clockwise? (_____)

69. In what direction is he facing if he makes a quarter turn anti-clockwise and then a half turn clockwise? (_____)

70. In what direction is he facing if he makes a three-quarter turn clockwise and a half turn clockwise, and finally a quarter turn anti-clockwise? (_____)

In each of the following questions one word can be put in front of each of the four given words to form a new word. Write the correct word in the brackets.

Look at this example: board   berry   out   bird   **(BLACK)**

71. mill   fall   shield   screen   (_____)

72. shot   less   thirsty   shed   (_____)

73. card   man   mark   master   (_____)

74. age   hole   kind   slaughter   (_____)

75. scape   mark   lord   slide   (_____)

The table below gives the time in seconds taken by 4 children to swim distances of 1, 2 and 5 lengths of a swimming pool.

No of LENGTHS	1	2	5
TOBY	23sec	59sec	218sec
BELLA	34sec	85sec	315sec
HARRY	28sec	70sec	256sec
MYRA	32sec	81sec	289sec

76. Which child swam 5 lengths the quickest?   (_____)

77. Which child took approximately 10 times as long to swim
    5 lengths as Harry took to swim 1 length?   (_____)

78. For which child was the difference in time for swimming
    1 length and 2 lengths the greatest?   (_____)

79. For which child was the difference in time for swimming
    1 length and 5 lengths the least?   (_____)

Six girls A, B, C, D, E and F stand in a straight line.

Neither A nor B is at the end of the line.
No one is further right than C.
E is beside neither C nor A.
D is beside E and B
F is one of the girls in the middle.

List the girls in order.

LEFT   80. (____)   81. (____)   82. (____)   83. (____)   84. (____)   85. (____)   RIGHT

TEST 09

SCORE _____

1. Which letter occurs once in the word GEOGRAPHY and twice in the word GEOMETRY? (_____)

2. Which letter occurs three times in the word FLUORESCENCE and once in the word BEAUTY? (_____)

3. Which letter occurs most often in the word BELLIGERENT? (_____)

4. If I add 8 to a certain number I get an answer which is 4 less than 28. What is the number? (_____)

5. Jane and Sally had 31 comics between them. Jane had 9 more than Sally. How many comics did Sally have? (_____)

In the questions below TWO words must change places so that the sentences make sense. Underline the TWO words that must change places.

Look at this example: The <u>wood</u> was made of <u>table</u>.

6. The did you go to why park?

7. The its ate all of horse oats.

8. Out the door opened the cat ran when.

9. There are a basket of apples in the lot.

10. He into the bicycle rode the wall.

11. Eat down now and sit up your dinner.

The table below gives some information about the addition of numbers in the left hand column to numbers in the top row. Complete the table.

	+	0.9	2.1	
12.				
13. 14.	6.8			8.7
15. 16.	4.1		6.2	

In each question write in the brackets one letter which will complete both the word in front of the brackets and the word after the brackets.

Look at this example: **ROA (D) OOR**

17.   BEL ( ) ELL.   18. DUC ( ) ICK.   19. FEA ( ) ING.

20.   ITC ( ) EAR.   21. EXI ( ) ALE.   22. CLEA ( ) URAL.

Arrange the following words in alphabetical order.

PUPPY   POETRY   POCKET   POPPY   POPPET.

First   Last

23. (_____)   24. (_____)   25. (_____)   26. (_____)   27. (_____)

In the following questions a letter can be taken from the first word and put into the second word to form TWO new words.

Write both NEW words.

Look at this example: THEN   TANK   (TEN)   (THANK)

28. GAVEL   SING   (_____)   (_____)

29. FOUND   BOY   (_____)   (_____)

30. SHORT   BEAD   (_____)   (_____)

31. DETER   SING   (_____)   (_____)

32. FLOAT   SHUT   (_____)   (_____)

33. RINSE   SAIL   (_____)   (_____)

34. TITLE   SACK   (_____)   (_____)

Complete the following sequences. The alphabet is printed to help you.

A B C D E F G H I J K L M N O P Q R S T U V W X Y Z

35.	EN	FO	GP	HQ			(_____)
36.	A	E	I	M	Q	U	(_____)
37.	A	C	F	H	K	M	(_____)
38.	BZB	EXE	HVH	KTK			(_____)
39.	CAB	FDE	IGH	LJK			(_____)
40.	WAC	EBU	SCG	IDQ			(_____)

The dates of birth of 4 friends are:

Liam   19.10.01   **Ella   3.8.02**   **Molly   17.2.01**   **Oscar   12.3.02**

41. Who is the oldest?   (_____)

42. Whose birthday is nearest to Easter?   (_____)

43. How old will Liam be on 19.10.08?   (_____)

44. In which year will Molly have her 6th birthday?   (_____)

45. What age will Oscar be on 12th September 2009?   (_____)

In the sentences below there are 5 words missing. From the lists A to E choose the MOST SUITABLE words to complete the sentences. Choose a word from list A to fill space A, a word from list B to fill space B and so on.

Underline the chosen word in each group.

Many (A) can be planted in the spring. They need to be carefully (B) to help germination. Moisture and heat are (C) for growth. (D) light will (E) the growth of young shoots and weaken the plants.

46.	47.	48.	49.	50.
A	B	C	D	E
plant	watch	helpful	Weak	help
flower	moved	essential	Plentiful	encourage
seeds	observe	bad	Sun	cause
things	examined	harmful	Insufficient	hamper
vegetables	tended	useful	Extra	develop

The information below is about 4 boys A, B, C and D and the hobbies they enjoy.
A and B are the only two who like both reading and football.
B and D are the only two who like both football and painting.
C and A are the only two who like both fishing and cycling.

51. Who likes football but not painting?   (_____)

52. Who likes cycling but not football?   (_____)

53. Which hobby does A not have?   (_____)

54. Which footballer paints and reads?   (_____)

55. Which cyclist like fishing but does not read?   (_____)

56. Which hobby is the most popular?   (_____)

In each line below, the first word can be changed into the last word in three stages. Only one letter can be replaced at a time and proper words must be made each time.

Look at this example: tide   (ride)   (rode)   rope

57. time   (_____)   (_____)   lane

58. weir   (_____)   (_____)   team

59. pack   (_____)   (_____)   rice

60. pint   (_____)   (_____)   lane

61. work   (_____)   (_____)   load

The two sets of numbers on each line go together in a similar way. Write the missing number each time.

Look at this example: (3 → 27 → 23)   (5 → 125 → 121)

(Cube number and subtract 4)

62. (81 → 9 → 7)   (25 → 5 → _____)

63. (12 → 24 → 30)   (16 → 32 → _____)

64. (7 → 49 → 50)   (11 → 121 → _____)

65. (72 → 36 → 33)   (40 → 20 → _____)

66. (4 → 16 → 21)   (6 → 36 → _____)

67. (15 → 30 → 20)   (22 → 44 → _____)

**£43.75 was made up using the smallest number of notes and coins shown below.
How many of each were used?**

68. £5 notes   (_____)   69. £1 coins   (_____)   70. 20p coins   (_____)

71. 2p coins   (_____)   72. 1p coins   (_____)

**Some letters from the words in capitals have been used to make other words. Underline the TWO
new words that have been made each time.**

Look at this example: **CONVENIENT**   <u>tonic</u>   video   notion   <u>voice</u>

73. PENINSULA   please   slain   usual   pulse

74. GEOGRAPHY   grape   prayer   repay   repair

75. RESEARCHED   chase   dream   scarce   heard

76. MANIPULATE   pulse   tulip   lament   altar

77. AMBULANCE   blame   learn   manila   uncle

78. CATASTROPHE   castle   roast   treat   stream

79. SAFEGUARD   feast   garage   feuds   urges

The following questions are about the numbers in the diagram.

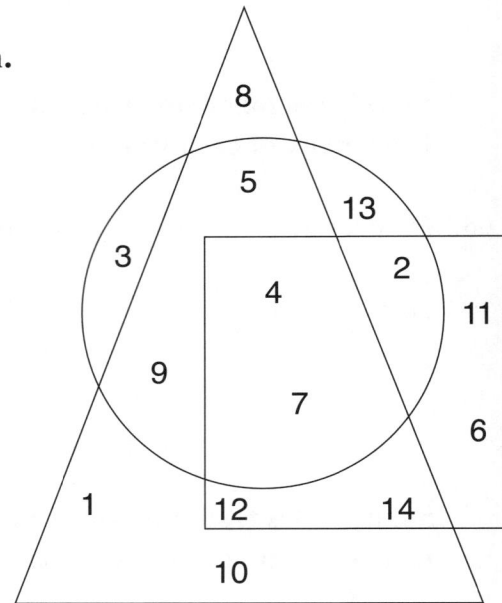

80. Which number is in both the circle and square but not in the triangle?

    (_____)

81. Which numbers are in both the circle and triangle but not in the square?

    (_____)

82. Which numbers appear in all three figures?

    (_____)

83. Find the sum of all the numbers which appear in one figure only.   (_____)

84. Take the sum of the numbers that are in the square, but not the triangle, from the sum of the numbers that are in the circle but not the square.   (_____)

85. Take the sum of the numbers that are in the circle, but not the triangle or square, from the sum of the numbers that are in the triangle, but not the circle or square.   (_____)

TEST 10

1. Which letter occurs twice in SUPPOSITION, once in SUPPOSE and not at all in SUPPER? (_____)

2. Which letter occurs once in BEDROOM and twice in MOMENTARY? (_____)

3. Which letters occur twice as often in BELONGINGS as in the word SONGS? (_____)

4. When I subtract 7 from a certain number the answer is $\frac{1}{5}$ of 35. What is the number? (_____)

5. Lucy has 3 times as many balloons as Mary and half as many as Pat who has 12 balloons. If Lucy gave 2 of her balloons to Mary and Pat gave 1 to Mary, how many would Mary then have? (_____)

In the questions below TWO words must change places so that the sentences make sense. Underline the TWO words that must change places.

Look at this example: **The <u>wood</u> was made of <u>table</u>.**

6. Do not from pages tear the books.

7. The girls park their bicycles to the rode.

8. The lights could and we fused not see.

9. May I door you to the see?

10. Curly pigs have most tails.

11. The teacher books the marked in school.

The table below gives some information about the subtraction of numbers in the top row from numbers in the left hand column

Complete the table.

12.	—	3.1	
13. 14.		8.2	
15.	4.9		2.1
16. 17.	6.5		

In each question write in the brackets one letter which will complete both the word in front of the brackets and the word after the brackets.

Look at this example: ROA (D) OOR

18.   SIL   (_____) ISS   19.   BOR   (_____) ARN

20.   MINU   (_____) IGN   21.   HEI   (_____) EADY

22.   DUS   (_____) IRED   23.   MEN   (_____) SED

In each line below a word from the left-hand group joins one from the right-hand group to make a new word. The left-hand word comes first.
Underline the chosen words.

Look at this example: CORN   **FARM**   TIME   **OVER**   FIELD   **YARD**

24.	CUT	BOW	PIT	LED	TEN	CHAIR
25.	GO	MAT	CAN	DYE	AT	SHALL
26.	CUE	ARM	PAD	ILL	BIT	OUR
27.	COY	CURE	OR	BIT	TONE	FEW
28.	AN	ME	DOE	NINE	ERR	AN
29.	PIE	SEAL	LINE	PIPE	BALD	THRONE

In the following questions a letter can be taken from the first word and put into the second word to form TWO new words. Write both NEW words.

Look at this example: THEN   TANK   (TEN)   (THANK)

The H moves from THEN to TANK and makes the new words TEN and THANK

30. TIRE   HEAD   (_____)   (_____)

31. SWERVE   TIN   (_____)   (_____)

32. HOST   EVEN   (_____)   (_____)

33. FRIGHT   HOSE   (_____)   (_____)

34. BELOW   FRIGHT   (_____)   (_____)

35. BEAD   POT   (_____)   (_____)

In each line below there are 3 pairs of words which change by following a rule.
Find the rule for each line and write the missing word.

Look at this example: NOT - TON   LIVE - EVIL   STOP <u>POTS</u>
The letters are reversed to give a new word.

36. patrol - tap   bustle - sub   nibble -   (_____)

37. cheap - pea   abate - eat   backcloth -   (_____)

38. gravel - leg   nectar - ran   bachelor -   (_____)

39. swath - sat   graph - gap   phantom -   (_____)

40. forget - ore   clout - lot   chapter -   (_____)

Two words inside the brackets have similar meanings to the words outside the brackets. Underline the TWO words each time.

Look at this Example:　　horse, pig, cat　(falcon, <u>mouse</u>, snake, trout, <u>badger</u>)

41. shoe, sandal, boot　　　　(feet, trainers, walk, wellingtons, socks)

42. steam, poach, boil　　　　(fish, fry, cook, roast, vegetables)

43. candle, lamp, sun　　　　(burn, torch, mirror, match, shine)

44. sad, gloomy, melancholy　　(unhappy, dreamy, tired, content, dreary)

45. daffodil, tulip, daisy　　　(garden, iris, beech, rose, cauliflower)

£69.64 was made up using the smallest number of notes and coins shown below. How many of each were used?

46. £10 notes　(_____)　47. £5 notes (_____)　48. £1 coins　(_____)

49. 20p coins　(_____)　50. 2p coins (_____)

Five children A, B, C, D and E went to school. B arrived punctually. D arrived after B but before A. C arrived early. E was last to arrive.

51. Who arrived at school at the right time?　(_____)

52. How many arrived after C?　(_____)

53. How many were late for school?　(_____)

54. How many arrived before A?　(_____)

55. How many arrived before D?　(_____)

In each of the following questions the word outside the brackets must ALWAYS HAVE one of the things inside the brackets.

Underline one word only inside the bracket.

Look at this example:　　　　**A MAN always has (wife, job, car, <u>head</u>, children)**

56. A HOUSE always has　　　　　(stairs, garage, roof, garden)

57. A CANAL always has　　　　　(barge, locks, water, holiday-makers)

58. A TRAIN always has　　　　　(passengers, cargo, engine, driver)

59. A BOY always has　　　　　　(shoes, limbs, bicycle, sister)

In a certain month there were 5 Thursdays. The 16th of the month was a Wednesday.

60. How many Tuesdays were there in the month?　　　　(_____)

61. What day was the 1st of the month?　　　　(_____)

62. What date was the second Friday?　　　　(_____)

63. Which of these months could it be ?　　　　APRIL, JANUARY, JUNE **(underline one)**

64. How many Sundays are there in the next month?　　　　(_____)

Amelia, Bella, Chloe, Daisy and Eva each have a new dress.
Amelia, Bella and Daisy have pink dresses, the others have green ones.
Only Chloe and Daisy have dresses with belts.
Bella and Eva have cotton dresses and the others have linen ones.

65. Who has a pink dress with a belt?　　　　(_____)

66. Who has a green cotton dress?　　　　(_____)

67. Whose green dress has no belt?　　　　(_____)

68. Who has a pink cotton dress without a belt?　　　　(_____)

69. Whose linen dress has no belt?　　　　(_____)

In each line below the first word can be changed into the last word in three stages. Only one letter can be altered at a time and proper words must be made each time.

Look at this example: tide   (ride)   (rode)   rope

70. farm   (_____)   (_____)   word

71. lime   (_____)   (_____)   tale

72. many   (_____)   (_____)   nine

73. sand   (_____)   (_____)   bunk

74. hard   (_____)   (_____)   cafe

75. lose   (_____)   (_____)   fast

In the following questions the numbers in the second column are formed from the numbers in the first column by using a certain rule. Put the correct answer opposite the arrow.

76. 1 ⟶ 2   77. 2 ⟶ 13   78. 24 ⟶ 10

2 ⟶ 9   5 ⟶ 31   36 ⟶ 14

3 ⟶ 28   6 ⟶ 37   42 ⟶ 16

4 ⟶ (___)   7 ⟶ (___)   60 ⟶ (___)

79. 9 ⟶ 4   80. 1 ⟶ 4   81. 24 ⟶ 42

36 ⟶ 7   3 ⟶ 14   36 ⟶ 63

64 ⟶ 9   4 ⟶ 19   47 ⟶ 74

81 ⟶ (___)   5 ⟶ (___)   68 ⟶ (___)

The graph below represents the journey made by a motorist one day.

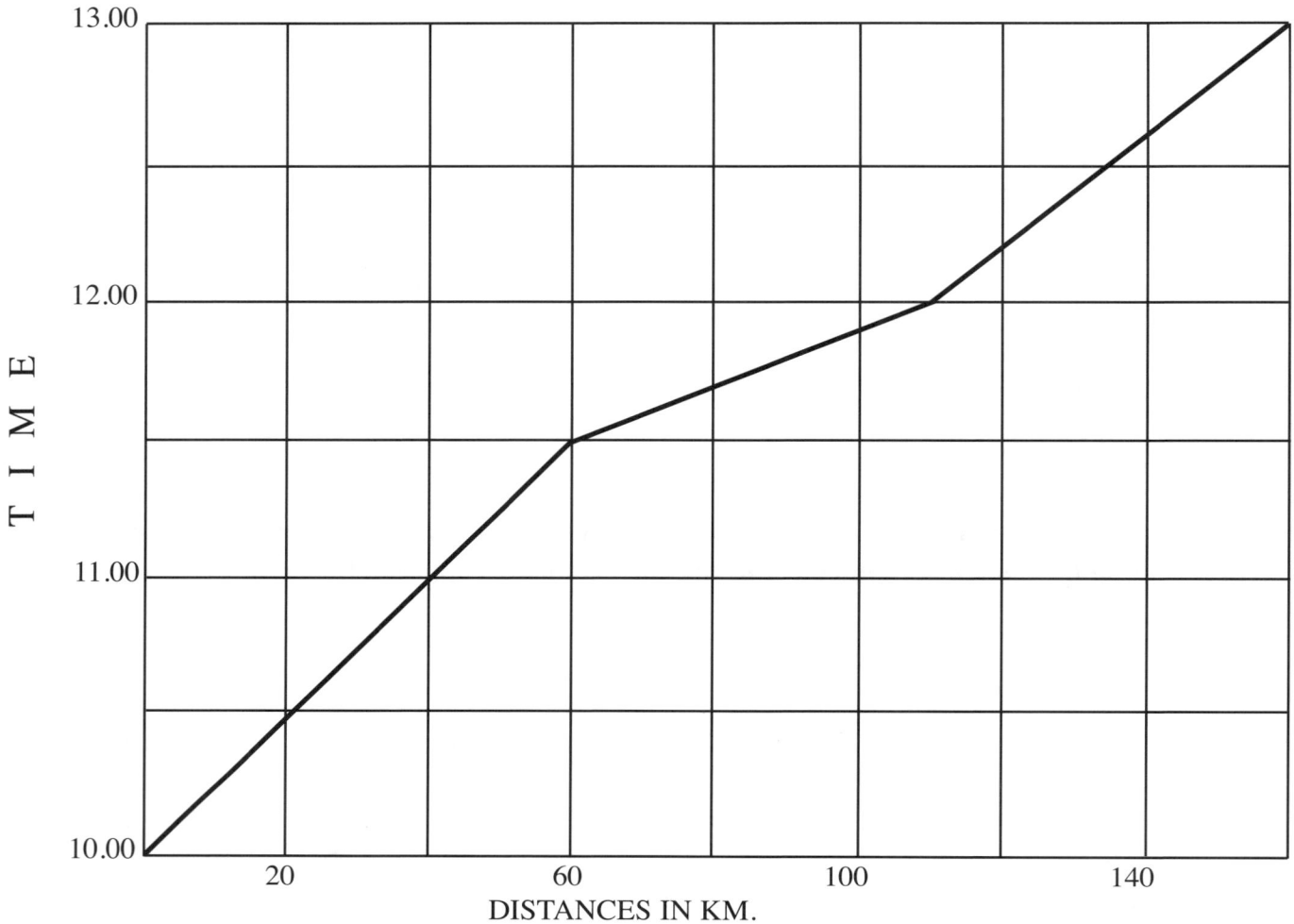

82. How far had he driven by 11.00 in the morning?   (_____km)

83. What was his average speed from 10.00 to 11.30?   (_____km/h)

84. How much of the journey did he still have to do at 11.30?   (_____km)

85. Part of the journey was along a fast motorway.
    At what time did he leave the motorway?   (_____o'clock)

Answers to Test 1

1. F
2. WEDNESDAY
3. I
4. R
5. CUCUMBER
6. ANCIENT
7. MOAN
8. BOAST
9. BUILD
10. SHY
11. GAS
12. LEAD
13. TURNIP
14. POUND
15. CUB
16. I
17. C
18. 23
19. R
20. 18
21. DOCTOR
22. CUT
23. PROFITABLE
24. PAUPER
25. ISLAND
26. SAMUEL
27. BEN
28. MAYA
29. THAN
30. WITH **
31. TO **
32. COVERED **
33. HAD **
34. WALK
35. CUTE
36. 3/4
37. 7
38. Q
39. 16
40. 6
41. £7.50
42. 7 APPLES
43. 50 MEN
44. 9
45. 19.5
46. P
47. 24
48. ER
49. WHEELS
50. FUR
51. FEATHERS
52. HEART
53. PEOPLE
54. TOP
55. BLADE
56. STEEL
57. SILK
58. SCARF
59. NAILS
60. SUBMARINE
61. HAPPY
62. WIN
63. BLUNT
64. FRIEND
65. OLD
66. UNDER
67. CRY
68. DRESS
69. DRIVER
70. HAND
71. WATCH
72. ADHESIVE
73. LORRY
74. THOMAS
75. WILLIAM
76. BLAKE
77. PURPLE
78. GREEN
79. SWEETS
80. SMALL
81. FLOWERS
82. 10
83. 1
84. 33
85. 40

FROCK
PILOT
FOOT
CLOCK
GLUE
TRUCK

** Other answers are possible.

Answers to Test 2

1. B
2. I
3. R
4. PERMISSION   CHILD
5. REGARDING   QUERIES
6. TO   ARE
7. RIVER   RAIN
8. WEEKS   LETTERS
9. B
10. A
11. E
12. D
13. 44
14. 17
15. 240
16. 489
17. 38
18. L
19. A
20. O
21. PQ
22. VJ
23. ILL
24. ART
25. MAN
26. PEN
27. TIN
28. PARIS
29. BELGIUM
30. HAMMER
31. THAMES
32. SPANNER
33. JADE
34. CHARLIE
35. BADMINTON
36. HOCKEY
37. GOLF
38. LENTIL
39. NOTED
40. NEED
41. OBSR
42. WRBO
43. TZWWOR
44. WATER
45. BROWN
46. STRONG
47. MUCH
48. SHINY
49. BEN
50. TEDDY
51. LILY
52. SAANVI
53. BELLA
54. SKIN
55. LOVE
56. SEAT
57. EVER
58. ITEM
59. STEM
60. U
61. R
62. Y
63. S
64. I
65. E
66. C
67. A
68. D
69. E
70. B
71. TEN
72. PAT
73. PEA
74. HID
75. LOW
76. D
77. A
78. A
79. C and D
80. MONDAY
81. D
82. A and C
83. 12/6/08
84. B
85. D

These are the answers to tests 1 - 5 of graded tests. A child who has not previously attempted questions of this type may have difficulty with the first few tests. However, research shows that a child's ability to handle and understand these questions generally increases with practice.

website: www.learningtogether.co.uk   E-mail: smcconkey@learningtogether.co.uk   Learning Together 11+ Publishers Ltd, 18 Shandon Park, Belfast BT5 6NW Phone/fax 028 90402086

1. A
2. S
3. I
4. 7
5. £1
6. SHOULD TAKE
7. CARS SPORT
8. WHITE COVERED
9. WORM BIRD
10. OF FROM
11. 9
12. 25
13. 26
14. 15
15. 24
16. P
17. Y
18. D
19. Y
20. R
21. BOY HOOD
22. HOME LAND
23. COCK ROACH
24. IN SIDE
25. BACK BONE
26. SACK WORLD
    LACK SWORD/WORDS
27. REED BEGAN
28. SOLDER GRAIN
29. HEAR DETER
30. HER DRAFT
31. MET
32. WAR
33. ROW
34. MEN
35. AGE
36. FLAG
37. PROFIT
38. AFFORD
39. GAP
40. SWAB
41. ALWAYS MANY
42. LIGHT HEAT
43. FORK NEEDLE
44. WRITE SWEEP
45. PAT EVIL
46. D
47. D
48. B
49. E
50. E
51. SPEED
52. NAVY
53. VISIBLE
54. SEA
55. TO-DAY
56. L
57. LLL£
58. LLLL
59. LL
60. LLLLL£
61. D
62. NE
63. SW
64. 180 DEGREES
65. 56 (X SQUARED - X)
66. 13 (X - 6)
67. 18 (X - 4) + 4
68. 128 (X CUBED + 3)
69. 31 (X x 2 - 3)
70. 80 (X x 2 - 20)
71. 0
72. 168
73. 2
74. 400
75. 834
76. 8
77. 100
78. PILE PILL *
79. WINE WING *
80. MINE MINK *
81. MILL MILE *
82. 3 5 7 9 *
83. 5 9 7 3 **
84. 5 7 9 3 **
85. 9 5 7 3 **

1. R
2. E
3. C
4. 48
5. £6
6. OVER ROAD
7. WAS THE
8. HAD CARD
9. TO THE
10. DELIGHT SKY
11. 7
12. 5
13. 12
14. 31
15. 13
16. E
17. P
18. L
19. M
20. H
21. AT TEND
22. FOOT PATH
23. BLACK OUT
24. FLAG ON
25. AT TEMPT
26. FLARE HERD
27. BEAN BRIDGE
28. BEACH EARL
    LEACH BEAR
29. BASS RASH
    BEAR
30. ALLOW BEEF
31. SUPERB
32. SUPERIOR
33. SUPERSEDE
34. SUPERVISE
35. SUPPLE
36. SUPPLE
37. 9.6
38. 36.36
39. 69.6
40. 32.4
41. HUNGRY
42. FRIDGE
43. TART
44. MOTHER
45. ANGRY
46. ANVI
47. ANVI
48. GEORGE
49. RYAN
50. RYAN
51. BE
52. HAND
53. BED
54. OUT
55. AIR
56. OVER
57. GRAPES
58. REAMS
59. RAPIER
60. IF-JHIU
61. QBQFS
62. TUBS
63. HOOFS
64. WET
65. SOLE
66. NAME
67. FLOOR
68. NEEDLE
69. 12
70. 16
71. 12
72. 8
73. 9 half X + 5
74. 55 X squared + 6
75. 480 10X + 10
76. 0 (sq root of X) - 3
77. 1 cube root of X
78. 42 (5X + 2)
79. <
80. /
81.)) /
82.)) <
83.))) <
84.))))
85.))) /

1. A
2. E
3. S
4. 40
5. 13
6. COLD RAIN
7. HARSH BIRDS
8. WINTER A
9. PUBLIC HOSPITALS
10. BUSH HAND
11. 12.7
12. 4.7
13. 4.5
14. 3.4
15. 8.1
16. D OR T
17. K
18. N
19. T
20. L
21. HOST AGE
22. IN AUDIBLE
23. SO UP
24. BE AT
25. MAN OR
26. INSET FRONT
27. MOTHS MANY
28. SHOE/HOES LEST/LETS
29. FICTION BREAST
30. TANK CHASE
31. C
32. D
33. A
34. B
35. E
36. SHADOW
37. PROTECT
38. EXCUSE
39. TREBLE
40. WAIT
41. FLEET
42. MELT
43. 4
44. 47
45. 1.1
46. 216
47. 103
48. 1250
49. 18.8
50. PEAL
51. CALLING
52. LIGHTLY
53. CHRISTMAS
54. DECORATED
55. 19 5X - 6
56. 24 X SQUARED - 2X
57. 28 $\frac{1}{2}$ of X + 6
58. 1.6 $\frac{1}{4}$ of X
59. 222 X cubed + X
60. 529 X - 9
61. SOIL
62. FUR
63. BUILDINGS
64. PAGES
65. FEATHERS
66. ROOTS
67. 24
68. 3
69. 11
70. Y
71. XW
72. XXV
73. W
74. PRQNHB
75. UDEELW
76. FINCH
77. CAGE
78. 2
79. 5
80. 4
81. 1
82. 3
83. $\frac{1}{4}$
84. $\frac{1}{2}$
85. $\frac{3}{4}$

* There are other possibilities.

** Other Combinations may work.

Answers to Test 06

1. T
2. C
3. 5
4. 28p
5. BREAKFAST SWITCHED
6. OUTSIDE BROKE
7. CROSSING WHEN
8. NOT WITHOUT
9. FOOLISH HASTY
10. 4.1
11. 5.2
12. 3.7
13. 2.7
14. 0.4
15. H or P
16. R
17. H
18. T
19. K
20. STAR TING
21. PACK AGE
22. BIN GO
23. MODEL LED
24. HOUSE HOLD
25. 64
26. 59
27. 72
28. 37
29. UNDER
30. OUT
31. TIME
32. SIDE
33. DAVID
34. CHARLIE
35. ADAM
36. YES
37. BEN
38. 18
39. 6.5
40. 4
41. 3.2
42. 168
43. 58, 37
44. CARAVAN
45. HOSPITAL
46. PIMPLE
47. LIGHTNING
48. REVERSE
49. ORCHARD
50. LAST
51. SPURT
52. AS
53. UNCONSCIOUS
54. CARRIED
55. 3 (X+8) ÷ 4
56. 125 (X CUBED)
57. 6   (X÷2) – 1
58. 121 (X÷2) SQ
59. 22   2X+10
60. CAULIFLOWER, PARSNIP
61. BOTTLE BOWL
62. SEEK EXPLORE
63. COACH INSTRUCT
64. EMPTY UNOCCUPIED
65. TRACE CRATE
66. GLOAT TAILOR
67. SLIDE PILES
68. TRAIN PARENT
69. MOUSE ITEMS
70. RHOMBUS
71. RECTANGLE
72. KITE
73. TRAPEZIUM
74. PARALLELOGRAM
75. F.BALL + HOCKEY
76. FOLK DANCING
77. COOKERY
78. COOKERY
79. 42
80. 7
81. 15
82. 19
83. 27
84. 38
85. 55

Answers to Test 07

1. U
2. I
3. 72
4. 23
5. 44
6. 10.3
7. 5.3
8. 7.8
9. 6.4
10. 5.8
11. BOOKS THINGS
12. ONLY IN
13. BROTHER NEPHEW
14. THE SCHOOL
15. LAP OVER
16. E
17. W
18. K
19. D
20. P
21. D or G
22. SCAR LET
23. THIN KING
24. UPPER MOST
25. PASS PORT
26. BE AM
27. 7
28. 1
29. 2
30. 1
31. 1
32. 1
33. LEO
34. JACK
35. THEO
36. SAM
37. BEN
38. WORKING
39. BREAKFAST
40. TELEVISION
41. BISCUITS
42. LIBRARY
43. CORNET
44. 31st
45. MONDAY
46. 12th
47. 5
48. AUGUST
49. PEAR PEER *
50. LAMP CAMP *
51. WORE WERE *
52. WORD WARD *
53. ETHAN
54. CANVAS
55. LOGAN
56. STANLEY
57. 1
58. G9J
59. OT
60. K
61. LFV
62. R
63. NMO
64. 99 X SQUARED – 1
65. 28 (X+1)÷2
66. 18 1½X
67. 8 SQ ROOT X + 2
68. YES
69. FIRE
70. EXIT
71. DIAL
72. FOAL
73. 18
74. 11
75. HOUSE
76. TILES
77. PITCHER
78. THRICE
79. KIJGAF
80. BFCAJGF
81. 6 6 4 7 2 **
82. 4 4 2 7 6 **
83. 4 4 2 7 6 **
84. 7 7 4 2 6 **
85. 4 4 6 7 2 **

*   There are other possibilities.
** Other combinations may work.

These are the answers to tests 6 - 10 of graded tests. A child who has not previously attempted questions of this type may have difficulty with the first few tests. However, research shows that a child's ability to handle and understand these questions generally increases with practice.

website: www.learningtogether.co.uk   E-mail: smcconkey@learningtogether.co.uk   Learning Together 11+ Publishers Ltd, 18 Shandon Park, Belfast BT5 6NW Phone/fax 028 90402086

Answers to Test 08

1. H
2. H
3. D
4. DIFFICULT TEACHER
5. THUNDER THE
6. DOG'S FIVE
7. BOOK RACED
8. TO SOMETIMES
9. SLEEP TIME
10. B,G,M or T
11. K or T
12. L
13. S
14. Y
15. H
16. 0.4
17. 11.3
18. 7.3
19. 13.1
20. 6
21. 26
22. 389
23. 39
24. 62
25. 39
26. BOAR
27. FORE or REAR
28. HIVE
29. MINT
30. AUNT
31. HERE
32. YEAR or EARN
33. CHAPTER
34. BORING
35. DEVELOPED
36. RESCUED
37. HELPLESS
38. 560
39. 952
40. £1.75
41. £3
42. PENGUIN
43. SHOULDER
44. VARNISH
45. MANHOLE
46. RUCKSACK
47. FAITHFUL
48. EVIDENCE
49. 5
50. 20th
51. MONDAY
52. 27th
53. 12th
54. 19
55. 162
56. 3.5
57. 6.4
58. 6.87
59. £12.50
60. £3.49
61. £1.70
62. YES
63. 8
64. 23
65. 3
66. ⅙
67. SW
68. SW
69. NE
70. NW
71. WIND
72. BLOOD
73. POST
74. MAN
75. LAND
76. TOBY
77. MYRA
78. BELLA
79. TOBY
80. E
81. D
82. B
83. F
84. A
85. C

Answers to Test 09

1. E
2. E
3. E
4. 16
5. 11
6. THE WHY
7. ITS HORSE
8. OUT WHEN
9. BASKET LOT
10. INTO RODE
11. EAT SIT
12. 1.9
13. 7.7
14. 8.9
15. 5
16. 6
17. T
18. K
19. R or T
20. H
21. T
22. R
23. POCKET
24. POETRY
25. POPPET
26. POPPY
27. PUPPY
28. GAVE SLING
29. FOND BUOY
30. SHOT BEARD/BREAD
31. DEER STING
32. FLAT SHOUT
33. RISE SNAIL
34. TILE STACK
35. IR
36. Y
37. P
38. NRN
39. OMN
40. OEK
41. MOLLY
42. OSCAR
43. 7
44. 2007
45. 7 or 7½
46. SEEDS
47. TENDED
48. ESSENTIAL
49. INSUFFICENT
50. HAMPER
51. A
52. C
53. PAINTING
54. B
55. C
56. FOOTBALL
57. LIME LINE *
58. WEAR TEAR *
59. PACE RACE *
60. PANT PANE *
61. WORD LORD *
62. 3 SQ ROOT X-2
63. 38 2X+6
64. 122 X SQUARED + 1
65. 17 HALF X-3
66. 41 SQUARED + 5
67. 34 2X - 10
68. 8
69. 3
70. 3
71. 7
72. 1
73. SLAIN PULSE
74. GRAPE REPAY
75. CHASE HEARD
76. TULIP LAMENT
77. BLAME UNCLE
78. ROAST TREAT
79. FUEDS URGES
80. 2
81. 5 and 9
82. 4 and 7
83. 52
84. 11
85. 3

Answers to Test 10

1. O
2. M
3. N and G
4. 14
5. 5
6. FROM TEAR
7. PARK RODE
8. COULD FUSED
9. DOOR SEE
10. CURLY MOST
11. BOOKS MARKED
12. 2.8
13. 11.3
14. 8.5
15. 1.8
16. 3.4
17. 3.7
18. K
19. E
20. S
21. R
22. R
23. U
24. BOW LED
25. GO AT
26. ARM OUR
27. OR BIT
28. ME AN
29. PIE BALD
30. TIE HEARD
31. SERVE TWIN
32. HOT LOST *
33. FIGHT HORSE
34. BLOW FREIGHT
35. BAD POET
36. BIN
37. HOT
38. ROB
39. PAN
40. HAT
41. TRAINERS, WELLINGTON
42. FRY, ROAST
43. TORCH, MATCH
44. UNHAPPY, DREARY
45. IRIS, ROSE
46. 6
47. 1
48. 4
49. 3
50. 2
51. B
52. 4
53. 3
54. 3
55. 2
56. ROOF
57. WATER
58. ENGINE *
59. LIMBS *
60. 5
61. TUESDAY
62. 11th
63. JANUARY
64. 4
65. DAISY
66. EVA
67. EVA
68. BELLA
69. AMELIA
70. WORM
71. TIME TILE *
72. MINE MANE *
73. SANK BANK *
74. CARD CARE *
75. LOST LAST *
76. X CUBED + 1
77. 43 6X + 1
78. 22 (X ÷ 3) + 2
79. 10 SQ ROOT X + 1
80. 24 5 X -1
81. 86 REVERSE NUM-BERS
82. 40 KM
83. 40 KM/H
84. 100 KM
85. 12.00 O'CLOCK

*THERE ARE OTHER POSSIBITIES